The Spirit of the Walrus

Elisavietta Ritchie

Elisavietta Ritchie

The Spirit of the Walrus

Elisavietta Ritchie

2005

Bright Hill Press
Treadwell, New York

Other Books by the Author

Awaiting Permission to Land
In Haste I Write You This Note: Stories & Half-Stories
The Arc of the Storm
Elegy for the Other Woman
Wild Garlic: Journal of Maria X
(a novella in verse)
A Wound-Up Cat and Other Bedtime Stories
Flying Time: Stories & Half-Stories
The Problem with Eden
Raking the Snow
Moving to Larger Quarters
A Sheath of Dreams and Other Games
Tightening the Circle over Eel Country
Timbot (a novella in verse)

Poetry Anthologies Edited

*The Dolphin's Arc: Poems on Endangered Creatures of
the Sea*
Finding the Name

Translations

The Twelve, by Aleksandr Blok

The Spirit of the Walrus
Elisavietta Ritchie

Selected by Bright Hill Press
Bright Hill Press At Hand Poetry Chapbook Series, No. 13

Cover Art and Book Design: Bertha Rogers
Editor in Chief: Bertha Rogers
Editorial Staff: Ernest M. Fishman, Lawrence E. Shaw

Library of Congress Cataloging-in-Publication Data

Ritchie, Elisavietta.
  The spirit of the walrus / Elisavietta Ritchie.
      p. cm. -- (Bright Hill Press at hand poetry chapbook
series ; no. 13)
   ISBN 1-892471-27-2 (alk. paper)
   I. Title. II. Series.

   PS3568.I8S65 2005
   811'.54--dc22

                          2005027918

The Spirit of the Walrus is published by Bright Hill Press. Bright
Hill Press, Inc., a not-for-profit, 501©(3) literary and educational
organization, was founded in 1992. The organization is registered with the
New York State Department of State, Office of Charities Registration.
Publication of *The Spirit of the Walrus* is made possible, in part, with
public funds from the Literature Program of the New York State
Council on the Arts, a State Agency.

Editorial Address
Bright Hill Press, Inc.
94 Church Street, POB 193
Treadwell, NY 13846-0193
Voice / Fax: 607-829-5055
Web Site: www.brighthillpress.org
E-mail: wordthur@stny.rr.com

[clmp]

Acknowledgments

Grateful acknowledgment is made to the following journals, magazines, and anthologies for poems that originally appeared in them, usually in earlier versions:

Blue Unicorn: "House Lions"
Canadian Writer's Journal: "Art Appreciation"
Christian Science Monitor: "Territorial Imperatives"
Confrontation: "Big Dog. Red Ball. Clear Skies"
Earth's Daughters: "Aftermath," "In Residence,"
        "Not Just about a Spotted Camel Cricket"
Fresh Water: Poems from Rivers, Lakes, and Streams:
        "Visitations, Procreations"
Kalliope, a Journal of Women's Literature & Art:
        "Lunar Gambles"
The Ledge: "Dead Hen Chronicles"
Muse-apprentice-guild.com: "Stag in Moonlight"
Oberon: "Chickens Are Not Emotionally Satisfying Pets"
Poetry: "Inua"
Potomac Review: "Terra Irredenta," "Visitations, Procreations"
Pudding House Press: "Terra Irredenta,"
        "Visitations, Procreations"
Quantum Tao: "Spotted *Rana pipens*"
Washington Writers Publishing House: "Territorial Imperatives"

The author wishes to express her gratitude for encouragement and help from the PEN Syndicated Fiction Project for four awards: the DC Commission for the Arts and Humanities for four Individual Artist Grants: The Virginia Center for the Creative Arts for several fellowships; the Washington Writers Publishing House; Dougald McMillan of Signal Books, Chapel Hill; Kevin Walzer and Jori Loredo of WordTech Communications; Keith Daniels and Toni Daniels of Anamnesis Press.

She also wishes to thank, for their editorial assistance and encouragement with this collection, Jorge Artamonoff, Laura Brylawski-Miller, Maxine Combs, Elizabeth Follin-Jones, Karen Green, Faith Jackson, Vivette Kady, Ann Knox, Phil Kurata, Judith McCombs, Jim Nason, Richard Rosenman, Elixabeth Stevens, and Hilary Tham.

Special thanks to Clyde Henri Farnsworth

for
Charles Alexander Ritchie
Elizabeth Anne Ritchie
Jessie Elspeth Curtis
Lyell Milford Curtis
Zachary Arthur Ritchie
Tyler Edward Rich

Elisavietta Ritchie

Contents

INUA

*"The Eskimos believed that the inua
of an animal enjoyed being hunted
with a beautiful implement."*
—William W. Fitzhugh
National Geographic Vol. 163, No. 2

The spirit of the walrus
yearned for the flung harpoon
to bear the finest carver's mark

his own father's tusk
to hold the blade
incised with lines and eyes

the beauty of the tool
made pursuit itself an art
death a pleasure

his *inua* would find
inside an unborn animal
a future home

HOUSE LIONS
—after an etching by Durer

Like St. Jerome, we need to keep
pet lions dozing by our beds, their paws
upon our coverlet while we're asleep.
Affectionate despite the claws,

in winter lions make ample comforters
(we lack the monk's thick warming cowl).
They lull us with deep regal purrs
and guard us with their locomotive growl.

Lions were smaller in the time of saints
or in the artist's eye that had not seen
real lions in savannahs, stalking, quaintly
feasting on fresh antelope, bloody, lean.

True, table manners aren't well-bred.
Housebreaking them becomes a chore.
But why stare at a long-dead human head?
You won't find your live lion a bore.

For when we meditate upon a skull
we only learn what's in our own.
We quickly guess what lions mull
while they lick our cheeks: *fine bones*.

Elisavietta Ritchie

VISITATIONS, PROCREATIONS

A real big mother of a snapper
impervious to poison ivy, briars,
lumbers up the river bank.

Shell slate black, crenellated at the stern,
snake neck, scaly limbs, hook claws.
That horny beak could sever fingers or a foot.

A dozen rabbits race about, skitter, bound,
zigzag, scatter among tiger lily clumps.
Still, I bet on her. She heads straight

across the yard, an armored carrier
programmed on a course set fifty years ago
when she was young, this lawn a forest.

She pauses on the grass. Confused?
Was there a house across her path before?
I offer her my pear core, sprint aside.

She studies me with loathing, mere disdain,
slow-stirred memory of a duel beneath
primeval cycads, or am I the perfect meal?

~   ~   ~

Yet she's hellbent not on war or lunch
but to unload her oblong leather eggs
in some cache underground. But where?

I edge behind, gingerly lift her—
not only dangerous, she stinks—
carry her to an abandoned flower bed.

She takes off, a millstone on the march,
around the yard's perimeter at such a pace,
distracted by the rabbits, I lose track.

She grunts through the herb bed,
crushes dill, churns the earth
between oregano and rosemary.

When I check again, she's covered up
whatever spot she finally chose,
slid down the bank and disappeared.

How did that repellent hulk
entice a mate so tolerant
of her appearance, scent?

~   ~   ~

Elisavietta Ritchie

Was he drawn by long affection
or, with pure chelonian lust,
snatched the first female to swim past

for lengthy coupling or quick fix?
Love in the muck in the dark
or light of the moon on waves,

to prolong her dynasty engendered
before dinosaurs were born.
Like roaches, snappers may outlive us.

Unsure of their gestation span, I'll watch
the spot, escort phalanxes of hatchlings
to the shore, ward off ospreys, foxes, gulls . . . .

But this very night, raccoons
search among the herbs, leave
shards like broken ping-pong balls.

Lunar Gambles

Whether to hang out the wash
or, given peculiar flickers of leaves,
my bones sensing rain,

sudden roughing of cove,
gulls fled from the Bay
massed on our pier,
birds know when a storm is due—

should I wait for tomorrow?
This isn't a great decision. So what
if sheets, shirts, underclothes,
get an extra rinse?

First, I must rescue the luna moth
newly hatched by mistake on the dock:
she might fall and drown.

I convey her ashore,
my fingers a dangerous cage.

Such fragile wings, flakes brush off
like pollen, dusty bluegreen,
the chrysoprase of tropical seas.

~   ~   ~

Elisavietta Ritchie

"Please," I beg, "just look! She is not
my usual, ugly bug! *This* moth is a miracle,
any moth or butterfly is,
and if it rains then where . . . ."

I bear her out. The salmon-pink
hibiscus blossom won't last a day
and a bumblebee already probed
its dusty throat, the stamens,
yet a moth could find a sweet lair.

I guessed wrong. She flies
into the huge willow-oak.
Inhospitable, nothing in bloom.
Still, a sound shelter from rain.

Then, a silvery turquoise kite,
she disappears in dark clouds.

Some philosophic conclusion must
wait, so to speak, in the wings.

Until thoughts crawl inside my wet brain,
like the moth I will risk everything,
as with love, and hang out the wash.

Big Dog. Red Ball. Clear Skies.
—for Harry Kerasides, MD

1.

The neurologist tests my mind
to check for tumors, stroke,
whatever might be messing up

my sight, asks, "Can you recall
the three things on my list
five minutes past?"

Simple givens, easy enough:
Big dog. Red ball. Clear skies.
I pass the memory quiz.

2.

Yet the dog could also be red,
the ball big, a storm could whip up,
and spin both through the sky.

Thunder could frighten the dog
so he cowers, feels small in himself;
the psyche is where size counts.

~   ~   ~

Lightning could strike the dog—
his jaws clamp, teeth pierce the ball,
destroy the essence of *bounce*,

melt the deflated mass,
ignite the dog in red flames—
his ashes already darken the skies.

3.
Molecules gavotte nonstop.
Even inside the brain
everything changes, or nothing at all.

Enough tests. I'll hang on,
cherish my imperfections,
cultivate second sight.

Some day I may perceive auras,
have visions of actual dragons, new planets,
an accurate map of Atlantis, see God.

DEAD HEN CHRONICLES

Half the poets I know
have their barnyard tale
of shattered innocence:

a superannuated layer
plump enough
for the hatchet,

a rival rooster
strangled and plucked
for the Sunday pot.

Grandma's splattered apron
caused my loss of faith in the gap
between flighty beast and dinner.

I was six, allowed to tend the hens
until my favorite red
scampered headless

around the yard
a feathered fountain.
Drenched, I fled.

~   ~   ~

Elisavietta Ritchie

Age twelve, imbued
with scientific curiosity
in Pennsylvania,

I joined the older girls
in the plucking shed.
They'd done it before:

long narrow knife
up the throat,
stab the brain,

cut a certain nerve
to release the feathers.
At least these hens

were hung by the heels,
their blood flowed
in a bucket.

I learned to kill,
unfeather, and gut
while we sang

~   ~   ~

Gentille allouette,
My darlin' Clementine,
home on the range.

I reached inside
my naked bird,
yanked out

gizzard, liver, heart,
limp spaghetti tubes—
"Don't pierce the bile!"

Might she still
harbor an egg?
My fingers groped

her hollows . . . .
Suddenly she squawked!
I skipped that fricassee.

I've grown, tasted
most things once,
given up hoofed beasts.

~   ~   ~

Now Dr. Steinberg
urges chicken stew
for my anemia.

Onions, garlic, stock,
celery, carrots, clove,
parsley, bay leaves, sage . . . .

Still, across stratosphere
and years, that cry from inside
resounds, resounds.

CHICKENS ARE NOT
EMOTIONALLY SATISFYING PETS

As I learned in a lone Malay hamlet,
final year of a marriage, fowl are not
loving, like cats, which he banned,

nor companionable, like the mutt
he got third-hand after I chased out
a midnight burglar while he slept.

Burnished auburn, emerald and gold,
the rooster strutted with audacity,
wattles wagged contempt for humankind.

The black hen might have felt
primordial compassion, for
day after day, no matter that

the door must stay shut,
in she'd slip, rooster in pursuit,
stalk upstairs, leave her gift:

one beige egg, laid on my pillow
or in my bureau drawer
left open by mistake.

～   ～   ～

Were these fertilized?
Could I have incubated them,
turned foster mother to a flock?

But I recalled an adage,
*Don't try to teach
your grandma to suck eggs,*

found my darning needle, poked
a hole in the narrow end,
gulped the rich and slimy life inside.

TERRITORIAL IMPERATIVES

He slips past me into the house.
First thought: one of those vixens,
rusty gray, from the far meadow
or a bold part-collie mutt
strayed from a distant farm.

"Good dog," I say, in a firm but
friendly tone. "Go home, *go home!*"
But this—*wolf*—is big, coat full
as if brushed by a furrier's hands.
How does one speak to a wolf?

On the mountain road—
rutted, strewn with rocks,
other empty houses might
be preferable to this.
But I am here, and he is here.

We both chose this vista:
bluegreen hills, a stream,
pond crammed with cattails, reeds.
Briars bloom across the fields,
boulders push up from earth's core.

~   ~   ~

Elisavietta Ritchie

Barns collapsed, roofs caved in,
car parts and tractors rust in weeds.
Where could be his source of mice
now cats have fled the farm?
Only feathers in the chicken coop.

As for the shattered house . . . . But the stone
is good, so what if plaster, chimney bricks,
and glass litter floorboards sagging toward
a mysterious cellar. His den?
Spring is the season for cubs.

I've brought a broom. But he
may think I mean to do him harm.
I rest the handle on the broken sink.
Morning's best to deal with dust,
wells and wasps, windows, latches, locks.

He halts between the front door
and me, like a stranger not yet sure
if he will rob me or, muttering apologies,
retreat and let me breathe . . . .
Neither he nor I dares leave.

     ~   ~   ~

His house, though my name's on the deed.
I take my sleeping bag and broom,
edge into the spare room, close
that door, and in the final light
delineate my territory.

Elisavietta Ritchie

In Residence

Winter: field mice move inside
our rented, hundred-year-old house,
gnaw new holes in every room,
every box of crackers, pasta, cereal, and rice.

Our manuscripts are shredded lace
for tiny cradles, winding sheets.
Despite the landlord's stern advice,
I set no traps or bait: *God's mice. . .* Now mine.

Spring: near the abandoned hen house
where turkey vultures raised their single chick
(ungainly, ugly, fluffy, anxious to make friends)
until the landlord drove them out,

now a six-foot black snake sheds his skin.
Translucent, whole, this goes on the shelf
with arrowheads, fossil shells, otter skulls.
Then coil by muscled coil, I gather up

the glistening prize. He wraps me in obsidian
necklaces and crowns. I carry him inside,
ignore the cowered guests, point him
toward the hole above the stove.

~   ~   ~

"Go for it, pal!" Unsure, he sways,
then catches on, tries the hole for size,
inch by inch uncoils his endless neck.
The final rubber tail flicks, disappears.

Seasons pass. Autumn: no more signs
of mice though further generations must have
   fled
bare, chilling gardens, sheds, and fields,
sought our deceptive shelter.

He surely lengthened, thickened till unfit
to exit any hole. Too satisfied to try?
Odd slitherings in ceilings, walls,
confirm his steady presence on the job.

I don't inform the landlord. Summer: we move,
he reclaims his house, keeps in tenuous touch.
"I've plugged old holes," he writes. "No
   complaints
of wintered mice." No mention of my snake.

AFTERMATH

After the black snake
glides into the bluebird house,
swallows his prize,
bursts the roof, wrecks the box,

he leaves on the lawn the nest
woven of moss, grass, down
plucked from the mother's breast,
and, glistening in the sun, his shed skin.

I have known men like this.

ART APPRECIATION

The spider on the tattered screen
bit the firefly right in half,
then to her surprise,
switched on the detached lamp—
and fled back to her web.

All night, from my canvas cot
I watched the spider rush
to turn on that cool fire,
retreat, return . . . .

I was six, that week in rural Illinois,
my parents visiting Laszlo Moholy-Nagy.
The artist not yet famous,
his cabin had no running water.
Mosquitoes swarmed the privy.

He offered me a drawing:
all straight lines.

I only wished he'd sketched
the broken moon
with the spider's silhouette,
ensnared the firefly's luminescence,
explained that strange blue light.

Elisavietta Ritchie

STAG IN MOONLIGHT

1.
Those old paintings
are romantic but hokey:
What stag would stand
long enough for his portrait?
And the moon *keeps* rising.

The painter can hold
only the *notion*
of a synchronous
instant of perfection
which seldom lasts long

and may in itself deceive:
always some flaw,
antlers missing one point,
a patch of mange,
the Almighty is perfect.

Or like Audubon with his birds:
the artist might have shot, dined on,
stuffed and propped up
some buck in his studio. The *real*
stag stands in the artist's mind.

~   ~   ~

2.

Here, in this twilight moment,
a doe and newborn twins
gradually, like tide, graze to the edge
of the wooden bulwark
against the sea.

Heads down, legs splayed,
they balance, outlined against
the moon, half-full, already up
but as if dawdling still
to dapple waves and fawns.

3.

If you, my love, could see
the fawns siphoning teats,
white tails flicking,
skinny legs trembling,
you'd probably say

Pity it's not a stag,
too bad the moon's half-gone,
and the night alive
with mosquitoes,
I must finish my book.

~   ~   ~

You can't waste time.
The deer filter through
bayberry bushes, briars.
The woods go black.
I slap at gnats.

4.
While trying to freeze
in awkward words
this long instant of perfection
am I doubling the moment,
cutting it into halves, or by half?

Yet like the deer
who will continue
eating our apples and grass,
acorns, flowers and herbs,
I am doing what I cannot help.

And because often you
would rather read about an event
than witness or live it
(tidier, cheaper, less risk),
someday you might read this poem.

THE BUMBLEBEE GAMBLE

—after Blaise Pascal

In case God does exist, it's a good bet to live
life on earth as if He does, you can't go wrong—

I head down the pier to check the trap,
a chicken wire cube, thirty inches per side. . . .
Will we have crabs for tonight?

Must release any strayed terrapins
and small flounders which often swim in.
I haul the rope . . . . Something furred—

A mouse under my palm?
No! Help! A huge bumblebee
two inches long, and I'm deadly allergic—

I drop the trap, fling the beast
through briny air into the cove,
retreat toward shore, chased

by invisible swarms—
Yet this bumblebee has not stung,
he spared my life, and here I

hurled him to his death.
A matter of his life or mine.
Slow down, bless whatever gods.

                ~   ~   ~

Elisavietta Ritchie

But there he is, paddling, all six legs frantic
against the tide, aware of his plight
if not musing on mortality,

too breathless to bargain as did one
fabled, hooked fish: "Please, if you spare
my life, I'll grant you three wishes."

I grab the long-shafted net, dip it beneath
the bumblebee's wake, scoop skyward,
run the net ashore, and flee.

NOT JUST ABOUT
A SPOTTED CAMEL CRICKETT
—*Ceuthophilus maculatus*

Here she is, in the sink again.
Could be this was only one
of her million siblings I nabbed

last night and the previous day
and, careful not to harm
the jointed needle legs,

antennae twice the body length,
carried to the door,
liberated into snow.

Perhaps that one slipped back
through whichever entry worked
in our sold-as-airtight house.

Or a lucky bird or mouse
nabbed her in mid vault
escaping ice. This fate

would be preferable, no waste,
no sin on my conscience if I,
or rather she, fed another critter.

～   ～   ～

She likely shriveled up with cold
inside her plastic exoskeleton. I
shiver now, but *she* froze in earnest.

So I am, after all, to blame.
Again I am confronted with the same
or a new shadow soul

hopping with what seem
plaintive rises and falls,
thuds against slippery sides.

Hard to capture . . . but do I really want to?
She does not sting or bite
or exude nasty secretions,

those tiny spined tibiae won't prick skin.
Her kind can't make disturbing chirps
though she may eat her lover up.

This leggy, sand-colored ghost
does no more than snatch a stray
potato eye, carrot peel or lesser bug,

~   ~   ~

whatever sustains such Olympian leaps
that compensate for winglessness,
with which I also sympathize.

I cup my hands, prepare to pounce,
but where she *was*
sliding around an instant ago,

now just the sheen of stainless steel
gleams back at me.
Nor is she on counter, stove or floor

(the linoleum's patterned, dark
for camouflaging vermin, dirt).
And I am relieved.

Elisavietta Ritchie

LIKE EVE, I MUSE ON HERPETOLOGY

I too like lizards, their climbing, clinging skills,
how they seem to sleep till time to nab a bug,
or sprint, quicksilver-swift, and disappear.

At six I bought chameleons at the circus.
When they escaped, I hoped that God did not
change them to snakes, but let them grow

to crocodiles. . . . In Malaysia emerald *checheks*
  caught
our insect hordes. I later rescued foot-long,
blue-tongued lizards asleep on Outback roads.

In Maryland, observing blue-striped skinks,
still I watch for miracles of metamorphosis:
a lizard shedding all, transforming to a snake.

Were I Eve, I'd munch the apple, beg the clever
lizard for another. Ignoring risk of severed limbs
he'd not regenerate, a change of lifestyle for us both,

he would oblige me with a peck. Yet he'd not lose
  out
on paradisiacal joys: Look! behind the boathouse

~   ~   ~

two black snakes unwind from a burrow hole,

entwine long necks, while unseen beneath the
    ground
their remaining lengths are copulating sinuously,
unencumbered by octets of legs, or any sense of
    sin.

SPOTTED *RANA PIPENS*

I stabbed a needle in her brain,
snipped deftly through the chest,
hooked heart up to a turning drum

overlaid with sooty paper where a stylus
etched mountain peaks,
persistent *hop-hop hop-hop hop-hop hop*

She was meant to feel no pain.
Yet legs and arms kept twitching:
in her muted dream *hop-hop hop-hop*—

Was she diving, leaping, fleeing?
My frog was female: I'd checked
cloaca, void of eggs. With luck

she'd spurted jellied strings in Lake Cayuga
and a male was close, before
a fine net scooped her up.

That was in Zoology.
I was nineteen.
The frog reeked of formaldehyde.

~   ~   ~

The handsome lab instructor said,
"Disconnect your hearts
when the paper roll runs out."

I slipped her flaccid body in a bin.
By now she's long disintegrated
in some landfill outside Ithaca.

Her tiny heart still pounds
in wild leaps of my own
hop-hop hop-hop hop—

Last February was my turn
to lie anesthetized upon a slab
while they cut my appendix out.

Suction cups and wires
connected vital innards
to recording apparatuses.

While the numbing stuff kicked in
what connected in my brain: *rana pipens*,
and my own, leapfrogging heart.

You Invite *Me* to the Bullfights?
—*for Bart McDowell*

But I've always cheered for the bull.
Outside St. Louis when I was three
my grandmother walked me past a field.
"Look at the pretty cow!" "*That*, Baba,

is a *bull*." She repeated the story for years,
imitating my lofty scorn.
Did her listeners think to ask,
"How would so young a child know?"

Not sure myself. My first edition
of *Ferdinand*, autographed,
omitted specifics. But a bull
without doubt is a bull.

His ferocious glare, the confidence
he can smash all fences and walls,
and that brazen dangling appendage
like a misplaced sausage or garden hose--

no wonder Europa was terrified,
and bore such strange babies.
He bursts into the ring, eyes agleam.
To amuse the crowd. He pretends

~   ~   ~

red cloaks turn him off, and he's annoyed
by those flung spikes and pikes.
Then he gores the bold matador,
kidnaps the adoring ladies—thrilled,

they leap aboard, ride off astride.
For however sequined, mustachioed,
what toreador could compare
with even a barnyard bull?"

Elisavietta Ritchie

TRYING TO TRACK LAO-TSE
—circa 604-531 BC

When water buffalos—horns scimitars,
moods volatile—lumbered across
my path in our Malay *kampong*
I followed as near as I dared:

perhaps the Immortal Lao-Tse
might be astride, tossing off wisdom
and verses to disciples who trailed
with ink brushes poised.

The villagers, philosophic about their lot,
recited *pantuns* as they rode,
left papaya rinds, loquat seeds.
The buffalo trampled plants.

Outside the electric fence,
in Maryland now, I watch herds
of Angus and Herefords graze the fields,
more docile, but nobody rides them,

not even a kid with rodeo dreams.
No scribes behind, I pencil my own
words on tatters of paper but leave
no insights for anyone.

TERRA IRREDENTA
—*Washington, D.C.*

A doe and fawn in the driveway—
two fox cubs play in the yard,
a pair of red-tailed hawks patrol
the ravine where again we find
crayfish, frogs, fingerlings in the stream
before the water flows into a pipe.

Long fled from this bulging city,
now critters reappear after rain
in pairs as from Noah's Ark,
then phalanxes, battalions, *armies*.

Crows caw, jays scold, rats squeal,
roaches and termites click mandibles.

Welcome, unwelcome—not their concern.
By instinct they sense our weak spots.

They *will* reclaim their ancestral terrain.
This street, once their river, floods,
the garden is forest again. The house
built on swamp pulls into itself.

~   ~   ~

Takes numbers to launch an invasion.
Numbers they have. Now they want
their land back, they want everything back . . . .

Elisavietta Ritchie

About the Author

Elisavietta Ritchie's books include *In Haste I Write You This Note: Stories & Half-Stories* (co-winner, Washington Writers' Publishing House 2000); *Flying Time: Stories & Half-Stories* (four PEN Syndicated Fiction Winners); *The Arc of the Storm; Elegy for the Other Woman: New and Selected Terribly Female Poems; Tightening the Circle over Eel Country* (Great Lakes Colleges Association's 1975-76 "New Writer's Award"; *Raking the Snow* (winner, Washington Writers' Publishing House 1981-82); *Timbot; Wild Garlic: The Journal of Maria X; Awaiting Permission to Land* (Anamnesis Award 2001), due from WordTech Communications in 2006. She has edited *The Dolphin's Arc: Endangered Creatures of the Sea,* and others. She teaches creative writing workshops for adults and students.

Her poetry, fiction, creative nonfiction, and translations have appeared in *Poetry, Poetry Anthology 1912-2002; American Scholar, New York Times, Christian Science Monitor, Washington Post, National Georgraphic, J.A.MA. The Journal of the American Medical Association; New York Quarterly; Confrontation; Press; New Letters; Kalliope; Nimrod; Canadian Woman Studies; Calyx; Iris; Atlanta;* and many anthologies, including *Sound & Sense; When I'm An Old Woman I Shall Wear Purple; If I Had My Life to Live Over I would Pick More Daisies; The Tie that Binds; If I Had a Hammer; Women's Work; Grow Old Along with Me / The Best is Yet to Be; Generation to Generation; The Muse Strikes Back; Beyond Lament: Poems on the Holocaust; Love is Ageless—Stories about Alzheimer's Disease; Gifts of the Fathers; Stories from Where We Are; Diamonds Are a Girl's Best Friend; Knowing Stones; Essential Love; Only the Sea Keeps;* and many other publications throughout North America

(cont., next page)

and overseas.

Elisavietta Ritchie has read at the Library of Congress, Harbourfront, Folger Library, Pittsburgh International Forum, the Writer's Center, and other locations in the United States and Canada, and overseas. Her poems have been translated into a dozen languages.

About the Book

The type and layout of *The Spirit of the Walrus* were designed by Bertha Rogers, as was the cover. The typeface for the text is Adobe InDesign CS Berling Antiqua, and the typeface for the cover is Adobe InDesign CS Book Antiqua. The book was printed on 60-lb. offset, acid-free, recycled paper in the United States of America. This first edition is limited to copies in paper wrappers.

Other Bright Hill Press Chapbooks

Poetry and Fiction Collections

Gobbo, A Solitaire's Opera, David Capella (forthcoming) $8
2004 Poetry Chapbook Award
Bright Hill Press At Hand Poetry Chapbook Series

Degrees of Freedom, Nicholas Johnson (forthcoming) $8
Bright Hill Press At Hand Poetry Chapbook Series

Autobiography of My Hand, Kurt Olsson (forthcoming) $8
Bright Hill Press At Hand Poetry Chapbook Series

In Late Fields, Steven Ostrowski (forthcoming) $8
Bright Hill Press At Hand Poetry Chapbook Series

Instinct, Joanna Straughn (forthcoming) $8
Bright Hill Press At Hand Poetry Chapbook Series

Walking Back the Cat, Lynn Pattison (forthcoming) $8
Bright Hill Press At Hand Poetry Chapbook Series

LightsOut, Tom Lavazzi $7
Bright Hill Press At Hand Poetry Chapbook Series

Possum, Shelby Stephenson $6
2002 Poetry Chapbook Award
Best Book of Poetry by a North Carolinian 2004
Bright Hill Press At Hand Poetry Chapbook Series

First Probe to Antarctica, Barry Ballard $6
2001 Poetry Chapbook Award
Bright Hill Press At Hand Poetry Chapbook Series

Inspiration Point, Matthew J. Spireng $6
2000 Poetry Chapbook Award
Bright Hill Press At Hand Poetry Chapbook Series

Other Bright Hill Press Chapbooks *(cont.)*

What Falls Away, Steve Lautermilch $6
1999 Poetry Chapbook Award
Bright Hill Press At Hand Poetry Chapbook Series

Boxes, Lisa Harris $6
1998 Fiction Chapbook Award
Bright Hill Press At Hand Chapbook Series

Whatever Was Ripe, William Jolliff $6
1997 Poetry Chapbook Award
Bright Hill Press At Hand Poetry Chapbook Series

Low Country Stories, Lisa Harris $6
1996 Fiction Chapbook Award
Bright Hill Press Chapbook Award Series

The Man Who Went Out for Cigarettes, Adrian Blevins,
1995 Poetry Chapbook Award
Bright Hill Press Chapbook Award Series

Ordering Bright Hill Press Books

BOOKSTORES: Bright Hill Press books are distributed to the trade by Small Press Distribution, 1814 San Pablo Ave., Berkeley, CA 94702-1624; Baker & Taylor, 44 Kirby Ave., POB 734, Somerville, NJ 08876-0734; and North Country Books (regional titles), 311 Turner St., POB 217, Utica, NY 13501-1727. Our books may also be found at BarnesandNoble.com and Amazon.com.

INDIVIDUALS: If your local bookstores do not stock Bright Hill Press books, please ask them to special order, or write to us at Bright Hill Press, POB 193, Treadwell, NY 13846-0193 or to our e-mail address: wordthur@stny.rr.com, or by telephone at 607-829-5055. Further information may be found on our web site: www.brighthillpress.org.

Elisavietta Ritchie

Order Form *(may be duplicated)*

Title_____ Quantity_____Price_____

Title _____ Quantity_____Price_____

Shipping & Handling_____SubTotal_____

Sales Tax_____New York State Residents, and where Applicable. Note: We cannot process orders without payment of applicable sales tax. (Orders of 3 or more, subtract 20% from total before sales tax.) Member discount (Subtract 10% from total before sales tax)_____

Ship to_____

Address_____

City_____State_____Zip Code_____

CHECK OR MONEY ORDER: AMT. ENCL. $_____

(total includes price of book(s), plus shipping & applicable taxes)

MasterCard____VISA___ Card Account Number_____
_____

Card Expiration Date_____

Customer Signature_____

Customer Tele. #_____

E-mail_____

Card-issuing Bank Name_____

Elisavietta Ritchie